EVERYONE CRIES
IN KINDERGARTEN

A Close Look at Sadness and Depression in America

Derrick Beech, MD

Votum Press

PART I

**Infants to elders
Crying through the years**

CHAPTER 1

Everyone cries in kindergarten.

Sadness is pervasive.

It is inescapable.

Regardless of the strength used to prevent, avoid, or mask sadness, it always seems to surface.

Its presence is unavoidable.

There are many faces of sorrow. It can express itself as having a bad day, melancholy, or anger. Despite the poorly placed façade, sadness knows itself. It understands that it exists and is uncharacteristically powerful.

Sadness is so assertive that it can bring powerful nations to war, destroy loving relationships, and even push a person to commit an unthinkable act – an act for which there is no return.

Sadness, unharnessed, can cause irreversible harm.

This book is written to demystify sadness, to bring this highly misunderstood emotion out of the shadows. This book aims to shed light on the idea of sadness itself and clearly define the spectrum of emotions ranging from a normal reaction to life challenges to the pathologic tipping point of clinical depression.

To truly understand the spectrum of sadness - a sad reaction to an event or situation, a depressed mood, or major depression - it is necessary to deconstruct each of these emotions.

The goal is to understand the major elements of sadness in order to create a path for returning to a happier and more supportive emotional space. Further, by clearly defining depression, the hope is that appropriate actions can be taken for those affected to get help.

The purpose of this book is to provide clarity and understanding of a rarely discussed topic. To prevent the harmful and potentially fatal consequences of living with this disease.

Associated with and often a consequence of sadness and depression is the tragedy of suicide. The connection between suicide and depression will be examined, focusing on preemptive intervention and prevention.

Everyone has or will experience sadness. Many will face the unfortunate consequence of moving beyond a temporary reactive emotion to florid clinical depression.

These pages will help ease the burden, lessen the pain, and create a path to wellness, peace, and happiness.

CHAPTER 2
Why do people cry?

Everyone cries at some point in their lives for a variety of reasons. Crying is a natural and healthy response to emotions.

No one escapes shedding a tear, regardless of how hard they try.

Infants, children, and adults cry for a variety of reasons. There are, however, several differences in tearfulness in babies compared to older children and adults.

Crying in and of itself is a normal and potentially healthy response. It can help to relieve emotional stress and tension, and it can provide a release for feelings such as sadness, anger, and frustration. Crying can also help promote a sense of well-being and can reduce stress and anxiety.

Social bonding and connection can be strengthened by shedding a tear. When we cry, we show others that we are vulnerable and trust them to provide support and comfort.

Crying can also express empathy and compassion and help strengthen the connection with others on an emotional level.

There can be tears of joy or sorrow.

As a response to painful or difficult circumstances or

crises, crying can be a way to process and cope with these difficult emotions and experiences.

Crying helps us acknowledge and process our feelings, thus making it possible to move through these difficult emotions or situations in a healthy and positive fashion.

The act of crying often involves shedding tears. Certainly, tears can flow with or without crying, but usually, the outpouring of tears occurs hand-in-hand with crying.

Tears serve many vital bodily functions and can have beneficial effects, both with and without crying. Tears can help protect the eyes, regulate emotions, relieve pain, regulate chemical levels, and promote social connection.

By allowing ourselves to shed tears, we can reap the many benefits they provide and maintain good emotional and physical health.

Despite this, crying in adults is often seen as a negative or embarrassing experience, and individuals may feel ashamed or embarrassed about crying.

This perspective can lead to the suppression of emotions and a lack of healthy emotional expression, leading to increased stress and emotional distress.

Why can't crying in adults elicit the same response as when children cry? Crying in children is often seen as a healthy and normal part of their emotional expression. It is usually met with a supportive and understanding response.

CHAPTER 3

Why do we discourage crying when
it can sometimes be healthy?

Despite its benefits, several cultures discourage crying, and individuals are often told to "suck it up" or "be strong." There are several reasons why crying is discouraged, including cultural, societal, and gender-based beliefs and norms.

One of the more common reasons that crying is discouraged is the cultural belief that crying is a sign of weakness. In many cultures, crying is seen as a sign of emotional instability and fragility. Those who cry, particularly men, are often viewed as less competent, capable, and void of inner strength.

This cultural stigma discourages individuals from expressing their emotions.

Further, these negative beliefs also prevent those needing support from seeking help for emotional difficulties. Inappropriately labeling crying as a sign of weakness can lead to a cycle of emotional suppression and distress.

Societal expectations and gender-based norms significantly discourage crying, expanding on the cultural and gender-based view of crying. Men are often expected to be strong and unemotional, whereas crying is seen as a sign of femininity and weakness.

This gender-based stigma can be particularly harmful to men, as it can prevent them from seeking help for emotional difficulties and expressing their emotions in healthy ways.

Beyond being viewed as a sign of weakness, certain cultures, individuals, or groups discourage crying because they believe it is ineffective in dealing with emotional difficulties.

Crying may be viewed as a temporary and superficial solution to emotional problems. These groups believe that more effective, long-lasting solutions to their emotional difficulties should be expressed rather than crying.

It is crucial to provide men with the support and resources they need to express their emotions in healthy ways. Support may include therapy, counseling, and support groups, where men can learn to recognize and express their feelings in a healthy way.

In addition, it is crucial to challenge gender-based norms and societal expectations that equate crying to weakness. It is also vital to promote healthy emotional expression for all individuals, regardless of gender.

There are also differences in the attitudes and beliefs about crying (and emotional expression) among different racial and ethnic groups. In some cultures, crying is a natural and acceptable way to express emotions. In others, crying may be discouraged or stigmatized.

Various factors, including traditional gender roles, religious beliefs, and social norms, can influence cultural attitudes toward crying. In some cultures, men are expected to be strong and stoic, and crying is seen as a sign of weakness. This tainted view can be particularly prevalent in cultures that value masculinity and self-reliance.

Some ethnic and racial groups may discourage crying due to historical and cultural experiences. Certain ethnic and racial minorities may have faced discrimination and oppression, and crying may be seen as a sign of vulnerability and weakness.

This perspective can lead to a cultural preference for emotional suppression and stoicism, negatively impacting mental and emotional well-being.

Cultures where men are expected to be strong and stoic and where crying is discouraged are found in many parts of the world, including Western nations, Asian, and Middle Eastern cultures.

In Western cultures, traditional gender roles have often emphasized masculinity and self-reliance, and crying has been seen as a sign of weakness.

In some Western societies, boys and men are frequently told to "be a man" or "toughen up," which can lead to the suppression of emotions and the discouragement of crying.

In several Asian cultures, such as Japanese and Chinese, traditional gender roles also emphasize stoicism and emotional restraint, and crying is often seen as a sign of weakness or loss of control.

In these cultures, men are expected to be strong and unemotional; crying is often discouraged, particularly in public.

Traditional gender roles and religious beliefs can discourage crying and emotional expression in some Middle Eastern cultures. In these cultures, men are expected to be strong and stoic, and crying may be seen as a sign of vulnerability and weakness.

Admittedly, we present generalizations regarding cultural attitudes toward crying and emotional expression, as attitudes can vary widely within a single culture. What is considered acceptable for one individual may not be for another.

Additionally, cultural attitudes towards crying and emotional expression can change over time. Various factors, including education, social norms, and personal beliefs and experiences, can influence them.

In the United States, cultural attitudes towards crying and emotional expression can vary among different racial and ethnic groups.

In African American communities, crying, and emotional expression are often seen as a natural and healthy part of the grieving process and a way to release stress and tension.

In these communities, crying may be seen as a sign of strength, resilience, and emotional depth and is often embraced as an important part of the healing process.

African American church services, crying and emotional expression may be encouraged and seen as a way to connect with the divine and find comfort and solace.

African American communities also have a long history of using music, dance, and other forms of expressive arts to express emotions and cope with difficult life experiences.

These cultural traditions of using expressive arts to release emotions and heal are often seen as an important part of the African American cultural identity.

Similarly, in Native American communities, crying and emotional expression are often seen as a part of the healing process. In these communities, traditional practices, such as singing and drumming, are used to release emotions and connect with the spiritual world.

Crying and emotional expression may also be

encouraged during traditional ceremonies and rituals, such as powwows, where individuals can come together to celebrate their culture and heal from difficult life experiences.

In African American and Native American communities, cultural attitudes toward crying and emotional expression are influenced by a rich tradition of communal support and collective healing.

These cultural traditions emphasize the importance of emotional expression and the role of the community in supporting individuals during difficult life experiences.

Nevertheless, in both African American and Native American communities, crying and emotional expression are often seen as a natural and healthy part of the grieving and healing process and are embraced as an important aspect of the cultural identity.

Like men in other cultures, African American men may face societal expectations to be strong and stoic and suppress their emotions, including crying. However, this is not a universal experience among all African American men.

The African American community's cultural attitudes toward crying and emotional expression vary widely.

While some African American men may feel pressure to conform to traditional gender roles and to be strong and unemotional, others may embrace crying and emotional expression as a natural and healthy part of the grieving and healing process.

In some African American communities, crying and emotional expression are often seen as a way to release stress and tension and are embraced as a part of the healing process.

In these communities, crying may be seen as a sign of strength, resilience, and emotional depth and is often encouraged as an important part of the healing process.

There is no absolute right approach to expressing emotions. Ways of emotional expression can vary depending on personal beliefs, experiences, and cultural attitudes.

However, some general principles can promote healthy emotional expression for individuals of all races and cultures.

First, it is important to acknowledge and validate your own emotions. Emotions are a normal and natural part of the human experience. It is important to allow yourself to feel and express feeling in a healthy and safe way.

Second, finding healthy and safe ways to express emotions is important, such as talking to a trusted friend or family member, engaging in physical activity, writing in a journal, or seeking support from a mental health professional.

Third, it is important to be aware of and respect cultural attitudes and beliefs about emotional expression and crying and to be mindful of how your emotional expression may impact others.

Fourth, challenging societal expectations and cultural norms that discourage or stigmatize emotional expression, including crying, is important. Promoting healthy emotional expression for all individuals, regardless of race or culture, is equally critical.

Finally, it is essential to remember that everyone expresses emotions differently and that there is no "right" way. By accepting and respecting others' emotional expression and promoting a culture of emotional openness and support, we can help create a more emotionally healthy and supportive society for everyone.

PART II
Sadness and Depression

CHAPTER 4

Crying and sadness - different from depression.

Mental health typically implies a person's overall emotional, psychological, and social well-being. Mental health is a complex and multifaceted concept. It includes factors such as emotional regulation, resilience, social support, and access to resources.

Good mental health is associated with a sense of well-being, positive self-esteem, and the ability to cope with life's challenges.

Mental health can fluctuate over time, and various factors, including genetics, environment, and life experiences, can influence it.

It is important to note that it is nearly impossible to separate mental health from physical health or external factors affecting a person's well-being.

It's okay to cry.

Crying and depression are both related to mental health, emotions, and well-being. Yet, they are different experiences with different causes and effects.

As mentioned, crying is a natural and normal part of human emotional expression.

Depression, on the other hand, is a specific type of mental health condition characterized by persistent sadness, hopelessness, and a loss of interest in life.

Crying is a typical response to loss, disappointment,

or other difficult experiences. It can serve several essential functions, such as releasing emotions, communicating feelings, processing experiences, and promoting physical and emotional well-being.

Crying can also be a sign of healthy emotional regulation, as individuals are able to process their emotions and experiences in a healthy and constructive fashion.

Depression, also known as clinical depression or major depression, is a specific type of mental health condition characterized by persistent feelings of sadness, hopelessness, and a loss of interest in life.

Depression is a treatable mental health condition with a range of symptoms. Symptoms may include persistent feelings of sadness, hopelessness, a loss of interest in life, changes in appetite and sleep patterns, fatigue, and difficulty concentrating, characterizes it.

Negative thoughts and beliefs, such as feelings of worthlessness, guilt, and hopelessness, can also accompany depression.

The major difference between crying and depression is that crying is a normal and natural part of human emotional expression.

In contrast, depression is a specific mental health condition characterized by persistent sadness, hopelessness, and a loss of interest in life.

Another key difference between crying as a manifestation of sadness and depression is the duration and intensity of the emotional experience.

Sadness is usually a temporary experience that passes over time, while depression is a persistent experience lasting at least two weeks or longer.

Depression is also characterized by a greater

intensity of emotional symptoms, such as constant sadness, hopelessness, and a loss of interest in life, compared to sadness.

The triggers for sadness and depression can also differ, with sadness being triggered by specific events or experiences, such as loss, disappointment, or frustration.

In contrast, major depression can be triggered by various factors, including genetics, environment, life experiences, and physical health.

Crying due to temporary sadness and depression are not mutually exclusive; individuals can experience both sadness and depression at different times.

Sadness and depression are different emotional experiences with often similar characteristics but very different causes and effects.

***

Crying, sadness, and depression are all related to emotions and mental health. Still, they are different experiences with different causes and effects.

Crying can be healthy or unhealthy, depending on the context and the individual's emotional regulation skills.

Sadness is a normal and natural emotion, but it can become persistent and interfere with daily life.

Depression is a more severe and long-lasting form of emotional distress, characterized by persistent feelings of sadness, hopelessness, and a loss of interest in life.

Sadness is a normal and natural emotion and a common response to loss, disappointment, or other difficult experiences.

Sadness can be a healthy and natural part of the grieving process, providing a sense of release and comfort. However, when sadness becomes persistent and interferes with daily life, it may be a sign of depression.

Depression is a more severe and long-lasting form of emotional distress, characterized by persistent feelings of sadness, hopelessness, and a loss of interest in life.

Changes in appetite and sleep patterns, fatigue, and difficulty concentrating, can also accompany depression.

***

Although sadness is a normal and natural emotion that is a common response to loss, disappointment, or other difficult experiences, it can sometimes go beyond the tipping point and become pathologic.

While it is normal to feel sad sometimes, persistent and intense sadness can indicate that the individual is experiencing depression. Understanding when sadness falls beyond the tipping point to depression can help individuals seek the appropriate support and care.

Sadness becomes beyond the tipping point to depression when it persists for an extended period and interferes with daily life and functioning.

Persistent sadness, hopelessness, and a loss of interest in life characterize depression. Changes in appetite and sleep patterns, fatigue, and difficulty concentrating can also accompany it.

Negative thoughts and beliefs, such as feelings of worthlessness, guilt, and hopelessness, can also accompany depression. Individuals with depression may also experience difficulty making decisions, low self-esteem, and lack of motivation.

Unlike sadness, depression is not just a passing mood and isn't easily overcome with willpower or positive thinking. Depression is a treatable mental health condition that usually requires professional help and support to manage effectively.

Some key indicators that sadness is beyond the tipping point to depression include:

1.   Persistence: When sadness persists for an extended period, lasting two weeks or longer, it may be a sign of depression.

2.   Interference with daily life: Depression interferes with everyday life and functioning, making it difficult to engage in work, school, or social activities.

3.   Physical symptoms: Depression can be accompanied by physical symptoms, such as changes in appetite and sleep patterns, fatigue, and difficulty concentrating.

4.   Negative thoughts and beliefs: Depression is often accompanied by negative thoughts and beliefs, such as feelings of worthlessness, guilt, and hopelessness.

5.   Difficulty making decisions: Individuals with depression may experience difficulty making decisions, low self-esteem, and a lack of motivation.

Sadness can progress beyond the tipping point to depression when it persists for an extended period and interferes with daily life and functioning.

Understanding when sadness is moving toward a long-term, potentially pathologic emotion, such as depression, is essential. It can help individuals seek the appropriate support and care and promote recovery and well-being.

Depression is a common and debilitating mental health condition that affects millions of individuals in the United States.

According to the National Institute of Mental Health (NIMH), approximately 7.1% of adults in the United States experienced at least one major depressive episode in the past year. An estimated 17.3 million adults in the United States had at least one major depressive episode in the past year.

The incidence of depression, or the number of new cases of depression in a given population, can vary widely depending on various factors, such as age, gender, race, and socio-economic status. Women are more likely than men to experience depression, particularly during certain stages of life, such as during pregnancy, after childbirth, and during menopause.

People of color, particularly African Americans and Latinx individuals, are less likely to receive a diagnosis of depression and less likely to receive treatment for depression compared to white individuals.

Older adults are also at increased risk for depression, as are individuals with low income and low socio-economic status.

The prevalence of depression, or the proportion of individuals in a given population who have depression, can also vary widely depending on various factors. According to the World Health Organization (WHO), depression is the leading cause of disability worldwide. It is projected to be the second leading cause of disease burden by 2020.

In the United States, the prevalence of depression has increased over the past several decades, and depression is now one of the country's most common mental health conditions.

Depression can significantly impact an individual's quality of life, including their physical health, relationships, work, and daily activities.

Depression can also increase the risk for other health problems, such as heart disease, stroke, and diabetes, and can increase the risk of suicide.

***

Depression affects millions of people worldwide. Despite its widespread prevalence, the exact causes of depression are still not fully understood.

However, research has shed light on several factors that may contribute to the development of depression, including genetic, biological, environmental, and psychological factors.

Depression is thought to be associated with imbalances in neurotransmitters, which are chemicals in the brain that regulate mood, thoughts, and emotions.

The most commonly studied neurotransmitters in depression are serotonin, norepinephrine, and dopamine. These neurotransmitters play a crucial role in regulating mood and maintaining a sense of well-being. When the levels of these neurotransmitters are disrupted, it can lead to feelings of sadness, anxiety, and hopelessness.

Research has also suggested that inflammation may play a role in the development of depression. Chronic inflammation can lead to changes in the brain and disrupt the balance of neurotransmitters, leading to feelings of depression.

Further, a person's genetics (familial association) may also play a role in the development of depression. Studies indicate that depression can run in families.

While genes alone do not cause depression, they can increase the likelihood of developing the disorder. In addition, studies have shown that stressful life events, such as the loss of a loved one or a traumatic experience, can increase the risk of depression, particularly in individuals with a genetic predisposition.

Depression has more of a familial association than a genetic origin. However, it is very difficult to separate genetic versus familial origins, and depression can have both genetic and familial components.

Genetic factors refer to variations in a person's genes that may increase their susceptibility to developing depression. There has not been an identified gene mutation directly linked to the development of depression.

Studies have shown that depression can run in families, suggesting that there may be a genetic component to the disorder. Genes alone do not cause depression, and a combination of genetic and environmental factors is likely to contribute to the development of the disorder.

Familial factors refer to the influence of the family environment, such as patterns of behavior, communication, and coping strategies, on the development of depression. Familial factors can also include depression in a family member, increasing the likelihood of developing the disorder.

Depression can have genetic and familial components, with a combination of genetic and environmental factors contributing to the development of the disorder.

Understanding the genetic and familial factors associated with depression is important in developing effective prevention and treatment strategies.

From a psychological perspective, depression is associated with negative thought patterns and distorted thinking. Negative thought patterns, such as self-criticism, rumination, and negative self-talk, can contribute to feelings of hopelessness and helplessness, leading to depression.

Depression is a complex mental health disorder influenced by various factors, including genetics, biological, environmental, and psychological factors.

While the exact causes of depression are still not fully understood, research has shed light on several factors that may contribute to the development of the disorder.

Understanding the pathophysiology of depression is crucial in developing effective treatment and prevention strategies.

***

It can be challenging to distinguish between depression and temporary sadness, as the symptoms can be similar. However, there are key differences that can help to differentiate between the two.

Some of the most common causes of sadness among American adults include:

1.   Life transitions: Major life transitions, such as retirement, divorce, or the death of a loved one, can trigger feelings of sadness and loss. These changes can be difficult

to navigate, disrupting a person's sense of stability and security.

2.   Work-related stress: Work-related stress can be a major cause of sadness among American adults. This can include job loss, job dissatisfaction, or workplace conflicts. Work-related stress can also contribute to feelings of anxiety and depression.

3.   Financial difficulties: Financial difficulties, such as debt, job loss, or unexpected expenses, can cause feelings of stress and anxiety and can contribute to feelings of sadness. Financial problems can also lead to hopelessness and a sense of being overwhelmed.

4.   Health problems: Health problems, such as chronic illness, injury, or disability, can trigger sadness and loss. Health problems can also cause stress and anxiety and disrupt a person's sense of stability and security.

5.   Relationship difficulties: Relationship difficulties, such as conflict, breakdown, or loss of a loved one, can trigger feelings of sadness and loss. Relationships are an important part of our lives, and relationship difficulties can disrupt our sense of connection and well-being.

6.   Social isolation: Social isolation can be a major cause of sadness among American adults. This can include feeling lonely, disconnected from others, or isolated from the wider community. Social isolation can also contribute to feelings of anxiety and depression.

7.   Political or social issues: Political or social issues, such as conflict, inequality, or injustice, can trigger sadness and frustration. Political or social issues can also cause hopelessness and a sense of being overwhelmed.

It is important to note that these major life issues can interact with one another and can compound to create feelings of sadness and loss.

For example, financial difficulties can lead to relationship difficulties, which can, in turn, lead to feelings of social isolation. Understanding the interplay between these major life issues can help individuals seek the support and care they need to manage their emotions and promote well-being.

Unlike temporary sadness or major depression, there is a type of transient depression that is thought to occur due to the fall and winter seasons. Seasonal depression, also known as Seasonal Affective Disorder (SAD), is a type of depression that occurs in a seasonal pattern.

This type of depression typically begins in the fall or winter months and resolves in the spring or summer months.

Seasonal depression is thought to be caused by a combination of factors, including changes in daylight and serotonin levels and changes in circadian rhythms and other hormones.

During the fall and winter months, when days are shorter, and the sunlight is less available, people with SAD may experience decreased serotonin levels. This neurotransmitter regulates mood and helps to control feelings of sadness and depression.

People with SAD may also experience changes in circadian rhythms and other hormones, such as melatonin, that can disrupt sleep and contribute to feelings of fatigue and depression.

The stress and isolation associated with the holiday season and the cold, dark winter months can also contribute to feelings of sadness and depression.

Symptoms of SAD can be similar to those of other

types of depression and may include feelings of sadness, hopelessness, and irritability; loss of interest in activities that were once enjoyable; fatigue; difficulty concentrating; changes in appetite and sleep patterns; and feelings of worthlessness or guilt.

While SAD is often diagnosed in people who experience seasonal depression for several consecutive years, it is also possible for someone to experience seasonal depression for the first time.

If you suspect that you may have SAD, it is important to seek support from a mental health professional who can help you to identify the symptoms and develop a treatment plan.

Treatment for SAD typically involves a combination of light therapy, medication, and psychotherapy. Light therapy involves exposure to bright light, which can help to regulate serotonin levels and circadian rhythms and can reduce symptoms of depression.

Medication, such as antidepressants, can also be effective in treating SAD and may be prescribed by a mental health professional.

Psychotherapy, including cognitive-behavioral therapy (CBT), can also help treat SAD and help individuals identify and challenge negative thoughts and beliefs and develop coping strategies for managing stress and depression.

In addition to seeking professional support, several lifestyle changes can help to reduce symptoms of SAD and improve overall mental health. These may include engaging in regular physical activity, maintaining a healthy diet and sleep routine, reducing stress, and seeking social support from friends and family.

CHAPTER 5

*Social media, alcohol, and drugs
may contribute to depression.*

A comprehensive review of crying, sadness, and depression would not be complete without including the influences of social media, drugs, and alcohol on an individual's emotions and the potential to cause depression or suicide.

Social media has the potential to positively and negatively influence behaviors and emotions, particularly regarding sadness and depression.

Social media theoretically provides individuals a sense of connection and support, allowing them to connect with others with similar experiences or interests.

The influence of social media can be significant for individuals who are sad or isolated. It can provide them with a sense of comfort and understanding. Social media can also allow individuals to engage in positive self-expression and share their thoughts, feelings, and experiences with others.

However, social media often adversely affect emotions and behaviors, particularly sadness and depression. Social media can contribute to anxiety, stress, and low self-esteem, particularly for those who compare themselves unfavorably to others on social media. Research has also shown that social media use can contribute to feelings of loneliness and social isolation, which can contribute to feelings of sadness and depression.

Additionally, social media can contribute to feelings of anxiety and stress by exposing individuals to a constant stream of information and news.

Social media's influence can be particularly challenging for individuals already feeling sad or overwhelmed, contributing to hopelessness and a sense of being overwhelmed.

While social media can provide individuals with a sense of connection and support, it can also contribute to anxiety, stress, low self-esteem, and feelings of loneliness and social isolation. These adverse effects can and have resulted in suicide.

***

Alcohol is a central nervous system depressant. While it may initially provide relaxation and euphoria, regular and excessive alcohol use can increase sadness and depression over time.

Alcohol can also disrupt sleep patterns, interfere with the effectiveness of the antidepressant medication, and increase the risk of alcohol-related health problems, which can contribute to feelings of depression and hopelessness.

Drug use, including illicit, prescription, and over-the-counter medications, can also contribute to depression. Some drugs, such as cocaine, methamphetamine, and ecstasy, can cause a sudden and intense "crash," leading to sadness and depression.

Other drugs, such as marijuana and opioids, can interfere with brain function and disrupt the balance of chemicals that regulate mood, leading to feelings of depression and anxiety.

In addition, substance abuse and addiction can lead to significant life problems, such as relationship difficulties, financial difficulties, and health problems, which can contribute to depression and hopelessness.

However, alcohol use and depression are complex issues that are often interconnected. While moderate drinking can have some potential benefits, such as reducing stress and improving mood, heavy alcohol use can significantly impact mental health, including depression.

Understanding the relationship between alcohol use and depression is important for managing both conditions and promoting overall health and well-being.

Moderate drinking is defined as up to one drink per day for women and up to two drinks per day for men. Moderate drinking has been associated with some potential benefits, including reduced stress, improved mood, and increased social connectedness.

However, it is essential to note that these benefits only apply to individuals who consume alcohol in moderation and do not have any history of alcohol dependence or other health problems that could be worsened by alcohol use.

In contrast, heavy alcohol use, defined as consuming more than 14 drinks per week for men and more than seven drinks per week for women, can significantly impact mental health, including depression.

Heavy alcohol use can lead to various negative consequences, including increased anxiety, decreased cognitive function, and increased risk of addiction and dependence.

There are both direct and indirect effects of heavy alcohol use on depression. Direct effects refer to the immediate impact of alcohol on the brain and mood. In contrast, indirect effects refer to the long-term consequences of heavy alcohol use, such as the increased risk of addiction and decreased overall health and well-being.

One of the direct effects of heavy alcohol use is the disruption of brain function and the balance of chemicals that regulate mood. Alcohol is a central nervous system depressant. While it may initially provide relaxation and euphoria, regular and excessive alcohol use can increase sadness and depression over time.

Alcohol can also interfere with the effectiveness of antidepressant medication and increase the risk of alcohol-related health problems, contributing to depression and hopelessness.

In addition, heavy alcohol use can have indirect effects on depression, including an increased risk of addiction and decreased overall health and well-being. Substance abuse and addiction can lead to significant life problems, such as relationship difficulties, financial difficulties, and health problems, which can contribute to depression and hopelessness.

Treatment for depression and heavy alcohol use may involve a combination of medication, psychotherapy, and support from a mental health professional. Medication, such as antidepressants, can effectively treat depression and may be prescribed by a mental health professional.

Psychotherapy, including cognitive-behavioral therapy (CBT), can also help treat depression, help individuals identify and challenge negative thoughts and beliefs, and develop coping strategies for managing stress and depression.

In addition, seeking support from a mental health professional can be an important part of the treatment process, as they can provide guidance and support in managing depression and heavy alcohol use.

This may involve connecting individuals with support groups and addiction treatment programs and working with them to develop a comprehensive treatment plan that addresses their unique needs and challenges.

***

Drug use, including illicit, prescription, and over-the-counter medications, can also contribute to depression. Some drugs, such as cocaine, methamphetamine, and ecstasy, can cause a sudden and intense "crash," leading to sadness and depression. Other drugs, such as marijuana and opioids, can interfere with brain function and disrupt the balance of chemicals that regulate mood, leading to feelings of depression and anxiety.

As for marijuana, the relationship between its use and depression is complex and not fully understood. Some studies have found that marijuana use can worsen symptoms of depression.

In contrast, others have found that marijuana use may have a temporary, anxiety-reducing effect. However, regular and long-term use of marijuana can have negative impacts on mental health, including increased risk of anxiety, depression, and addiction.

It is important to note that drug use should not be used to self-medicate for depression. While drugs may provide temporary relief from the symptoms of depression, they can also lead to a range of negative consequences, including addiction and dependence, decreased cognitive function, and increased risk of mental health problems.

Drug use can contribute to the development of depression and can worsen existing symptoms of depression.

It is important to seek support from a mental health professional if you are experiencing symptoms of depression and have a history of drug use, as they can help you to develop a comprehensive treatment plan that addresses both your drug use and your depression.

****

Cannabidiol (CBD) is a compound found in the cannabis plant that has gained popularity as a potential treatment for various mental health conditions, including depression. However, the evidence supporting the use of CBD for depression is limited, and more research is needed to understand its potential as a treatment fully.

While some preliminary studies have suggested that CBD may have anti-anxiety and antidepressant effects, the results are mixed. More research is needed to confirm these findings.

Additionally, CBD's long-term safety and effectiveness for depression are not yet known.

Currently, most of the research on the use of CBD for depression is preclinical, meaning it has been conducted in animal models or in vitro.

Some studies have suggested that CBD may have anti-anxiety and antidepressant effects. However, the results are mixed, and more research is needed to confirm these findings.

There have also been a few small clinical trials that have investigated the use of CBD for depression. However, the results of these trials are inconclusive, and more research is needed to determine the efficacy of CBD for depression.

The results of clinical trials investigating the use of cannabidiol (CBD) for depression have been inconclusive. While some small studies have suggested that CBD may have anti-anxiety and antidepressant effects, the results are mixed, and more research is needed to fully understand the potential of CBD as a treatment for depression.

One study published in the Journal of Clinical Psychology found that a combination of CBD and THC, another compound found in the cannabis plant, was effective in reducing symptoms of anxiety and depression in a small group of individuals with mood disorders. However, this study had a small sample size, and more research is needed to confirm these findings.

Another study published in the Journal of Clinical Psychiatry found that CBD was not effective in reducing symptoms of depression in a small group of individuals with major depressive disorder.

It is important to note that the sample sizes of these studies were small and larger, well-designed clinical trials are needed to determine the efficacy of CBD for depression. Additionally, CBD's long-term safety and effectiveness for depression are not yet known.

The results of clinical trials investigating the use of CBD for depression have been inconclusive, and more research is needed to understand its potential as a treatment for depression fully.

If you are considering using CBD for depression, it is important to talk to your healthcare provider, who can help you to weigh the potential benefits and risks and determine if it is a safe and appropriate treatment option for you.

It is also important to note that CBD products are not regulated by the Food and Drug Administration (FDA), and the quality and purity of these products can vary greatly. Some CBD products may contain harmful contaminants. It is important to seek out products tested and verified by a third-party laboratory.

The evidence supporting the use of CBD for depression is limited, and more research is needed to fully understand its potential as a treatment. While some preliminary studies have suggested that CBD may have anti-anxiety and antidepressant effects, the long-term safety and effectiveness of using CBD for depression are not yet known.

CHAPTER 6
Demographic and Socioeconomic factors associated with depression.

Depression is a common and debilitating mental health condition that affects millions of individuals in the United States. According to the National Institute of Mental Health (NIMH), approximately 7.1% of adults in the United States experienced at least one major depressive episode in the past year. An estimated 17.3 million adults in the United States had at least one major depressive episode in the past year.

The incidence of depression, or the number of new cases of depression in a given population, can vary widely depending on various factors, such as age, gender, race, and socioeconomic status.

Women are more likely than men to experience depression, particularly during certain stages of life, such as during pregnancy, after childbirth, and during menopause.

People of color, particularly African Americans and Latinx individuals, are less likely to receive a diagnosis of depression and less likely to receive treatment for depression compared to white individuals. Older adults are also at increased risk for depression, as are individuals with low income and low socioeconomic status.

The prevalence of depression, or the proportion of

individuals in a given population who have depression, can also vary widely depending on various factors. According to the World Health Organization (WHO), depression is the leading cause of disability worldwide. It is projected to be the second leading cause of disease burden by 2020.

In the United States, the prevalence of depression has increased over the past several decades, and depression is now one of the country's most common mental health conditions.

Depression can significantly impact an individual's quality of life, including their physical health, relationships, work, and daily activities. Depression can also increase the risk for other health problems, such as heart disease, stroke, and diabetes, and can increase the risk of suicide.

The incidence and prevalence of depression can vary widely depending on various factors, such as age, gender, race, and socioeconomic status. By increasing access to mental health resources and reducing barriers to care, we can work to improve the emotional well-being of all individuals and prevent depression.

Studies have shown that depression affects individuals of all races, ethnicities, and demographics. However, research has also indicated that specific populations may be at higher risk for depression.

Women are more likely than men to experience depression, particularly during certain stages of life, such as during pregnancy, after childbirth, and during menopause.

Research has shown that people of color, particularly African Americans and Latinx individuals, are less likely to receive a diagnosis of depression and less likely to receive treatment for depression compared to white individuals.

Depression is underdiagnosed in African Americans for several reasons, including:

1.		Stigma: African Americans may be less likely to seek help for mental health problems due to stigma and cultural beliefs that view mental health conditions as a sign of weakness or a personal failure.

2.		Lack of access to care: African Americans may have limited access to mental health resources due to poverty, lack of insurance, and geographic barriers.

3.		Misperceptions: African Americans may not be aware of the symptoms of depression or may believe that depression is not an actual medical condition.

4.		Bias in the healthcare system: African Americans may experience bias in the healthcare system, including discrimination and lack of culturally competent care, which can make them less likely to seek help for mental health problems.

5.		Underserved populations: African Americans are often part of underserved populations, such as rural communities, that may have limited access to mental health resources.

6.		Co-occurring conditions: African Americans may be more likely to experience co-occurring conditions, such as poverty, stress, and chronic health problems, which can make it more challenging to diagnose and treat depression.

By addressing these disparities and increasing access to mental health resources, we can work to improve the emotional well-being of all individuals and prevent depression.

To improve the accurate and timely diagnosis of depression in African Americans, several steps can be taken, including:

1.   Education and awareness: Providing education and awareness about depression, including its symptoms, causes, and treatments, can help African Americans recognize the signs of depression and seek help when needed.

2.   Cultural competence: Training healthcare providers to be culturally competent, including understanding the unique experiences and challenges faced by African Americans, can help to reduce bias and improve the quality of care for African Americans.

3.   Access to care: Increasing access to mental health resources, including affordable and accessible mental health services, can help African Americans to seek help for depression when needed.

4.   Collaboration with community organizations: Working with community organizations, such as churches, schools, and community centers, can help to reach African Americans who may be less likely to seek help for mental health problems.

5.   Integration of mental health services: Integrating mental health services into primary care, such as through co-located clinics or integrated care teams, can help to improve access to mental health resources and improve the quality of care for African Americans.

6.   Reduction of stigma: Reducing the stigma associated with mental health problems, including through media campaigns, community events, and public speaking engagements, can help African Americans feel more comfortable seeking help for depression.

By addressing these challenges and increasing access to mental health resources, we can work to improve the emotional well-being of all individuals and prevent depression.

Similar to African Americans, depression can be underdiagnosed in the Hispanic population in the United States. Cultural and language barriers and a lack of access to mental health services can make it difficult for individuals in the Hispanic community to receive a timely and accurate diagnosis of depression.

Studies have found that Hispanic individuals are less likely to seek help for mental health issues and may not recognize the symptoms of depression as a treatable medical condition. Additionally, cultural beliefs about mental health, stigma, and shame can prevent individuals from seeking help.

Language barriers can also pose a challenge for Hispanic individuals seeking mental health services, as they may be unable to communicate their symptoms effectively or access mental health resources in their preferred language.

Depression can be underdiagnosed in the Hispanic population in the United States due to cultural and language barriers and a lack of access to mental health services. Addressing these barriers and increasing access to culturally sensitive mental health services is important in improving the accuracy and timeliness of depression diagnosis in the Hispanic community.

***

Depression is a common mental health condition among older adults and is associated with increased risk for physical health problems, cognitive decline, and death.

Depression is a common mental health condition affecting millions worldwide, and its rates tend to increase with age. The reasons for this increase are complex and multifaceted and can include a combination of biological, psychological, and social factors.

One of the primary biological factors that can contribute to the increase in depression rates with age is the decline in brain function and neurotransmitter production. As we age, our brain function tends to decline, which can result in changes in mood and cognitive function. Additionally, the production of neurotransmitters, such as serotonin, dopamine, and norepinephrine, which play a crucial role in regulating mood, also decreases with age. This reduction in neurotransmitter production can result in symptoms of depression, such as feelings of sadness, fatigue, and difficulty concentrating.

Neurotransmitters are chemical messengers that play a crucial role in regulating mood, behavior, and cognitive function. In particular, neurotransmitters such as serotonin, dopamine, and norepinephrine are essential for maintaining a healthy and stable mood and have been shown to protect against depression. However, these neurotransmitters tend to decrease with age, which can increase the risk of depression.

One of the primary reasons for the decline in neurotransmitter production with age is the reduction in neurogenesis or the growth and development of new neurons.

As we age, the production of new neurons slows, which can result in a decline in neurotransmitter production. Additionally, the reduction in neurogenesis can reduce the number of receptors available to receive neurotransmitters, which can lead to changes in mood and cognitive function.

Another factor contributing to the decline in neurotransmitter production with age is oxidative stress or damage to cells and tissues caused by free radicals. Free radicals are unstable molecules that can damage cells and tissues and can result in a decline in neurotransmitter production.

Additionally, oxidative stress can reduce the number of neurotransmitter receptors, which can lead to changes in mood and cognitive function.

Aging can also affect the hypothalamic-pituitary-adrenal (HPA) axis, which is the system responsible for regulating stress and mood. The HPA axis is regulated by cortisol, a hormone produced by the adrenal glands in response to stress.

The HPA axis becomes less responsive to cortisol as we age, which can result in changes in mood and cognitive function. Additionally, the decline in HPA axis function can reduce neurotransmitter production, which can increase the risk of depression.

Finally, aging can also result in a decline in physical and mental health, increasing the risk of depression. Older adults are more likely to experience physical health problems, such as chronic pain, which can contribute to feelings of sadness, fatigue, and difficulty concentrating.

Additionally, older adults are more likely to experience cognitive decline, which can result in feelings of confusion and disorientation and can increase the risk of depression.

Neurotransmitters that protect against depression tend to decrease with age due to a combination of factors, including the reduction in neurogenesis, oxidative stress, changes in the HPA axis, and a decline in physical and mental health.

Addressing these factors and providing support and resources for older adults is important in reducing the risk of depression and improving mental health in later life.

Psychological factors can also contribute to the increase in depression rates with age. Older adults are more likely to experience significant life events, such as losing a spouse, friends, or other loved ones, leading to loneliness, isolation, and sadness.

Additionally, older adults may experience feelings of hopelessness and helplessness due to a loss of independence and physical abilities. These feelings can contribute to the development of depression.

Social factors, such as poverty, social isolation, and a lack of access to health care, can also contribute to the increase in depression rates with age. Older adults are more likely to live in poverty, which can result in a lack of access to adequate healthcare and mental health services.

Older adults are more likely to experience social isolation due to the loss of social connections, which can result in feelings of loneliness and depression.

It is important to address these factors and provide support and resources for older adults to reduce the incidence of depression. This can include increasing access to mental health services, providing social support, and addressing poverty and social isolation.

Depression rates tend to increase with age due to a combination of biological, psychological, and social factors. Addressing these factors and providing support and resources for older adults is crucial in reducing the incidence of depression and improving the quality of life for older adults.

***

Individuals with low income and socioeconomic status may be at increased risk for depression due to financial stress, limited access to resources, and other life stressors.

Several studies have shown that low-income individuals have a higher risk of depression than those with higher incomes. This relationship between poverty and depression has been well documented and is an important issue that requires attention and intervention.

A high-quality study that highlights this relationship is the National Comorbidity Survey, which found that individuals with lower incomes were more likely to experience symptoms of depression compared to those with higher incomes.

The study found that individuals with lower incomes were more likely to experience feelings of sadness, hopelessness, and fatigue and were also more likely to report difficulty sleeping and concentrating.

Another study that highlights the relationship between poverty and depression is the National Health and Nutrition Examination Survey, which found that individuals with lower incomes were more likely to experience symptoms of depression compared to those with higher incomes.

The study found that individuals with lower incomes were more likely to experience feelings of sadness, hopelessness, and fatigue and were also more likely to report difficulty sleeping and concentrating.

Finally, a study conducted by the World Health Organization found that individuals living in poverty were more likely to experience depression compared to those with higher incomes.

The study found that poverty was associated with various mental health problems, including depression, anxiety, and stress. Individuals living in poverty were more likely to experience feelings of hopelessness, helplessness, and isolation.

Several studies demonstrate that low-income individuals have a higher risk of depression than those with higher incomes.

The relationship between poverty and depression is complex and multifactorial. It is likely due to a combination of factors, including lack of access to basic necessities, social isolation, and stressful life events.

Addressing these factors and providing support and resources for individuals living in poverty is essential in reducing the risk of depression and improving mental health.

***

Individuals with chronic health conditions, such as diabetes, heart disease, and arthritis, are at increased risk for depression due to the impact of the health condition on their daily life and overall well-being.

Chronic disease is a major health issue that affects millions of individuals worldwide. It is associated with a higher risk of depression. Chronic diseases are long-term conditions that persist over time and can impact physical, psychological, and social well-being.

Depression is a common and serious mental health disorder characterized by sadness, hopelessness, and a loss of interest in activities. The relationship between chronic disease and depression is complex and multi-factorial. It can have a significant impact on an individual's quality of life.

One of the primary reasons for the relationship between chronic disease and depression is the physical and psychological burden of the disease.

Chronic conditions can result in physical limitations, pain, and disability, contributing to sadness, hopelessness, and fatigue. Additionally, chronic diseases can result in a loss of independence, which can result in feelings of helplessness and a loss of control.

Another factor that contributes to the relationship between chronic disease and depression is the impact of the disease on social and emotional functioning.

Chronic diseases can result in social isolation, as individuals may have difficulty participating in social activities or feel embarrassed or ashamed of their condition.

Additionally, chronic diseases can result in emotional distress, as individuals may struggle with guilt, shame, and anxiety.

A third factor contributing to the relationship between chronic disease and depression is the impact of the illness on financial well-being.

Chronic diseases can result in high medical bills, loss of income, and difficulty paying for basic necessities, resulting in financial stress and feelings of hopelessness and helplessness.

Finally, chronic diseases can also impact the individual's sense of identity and self-worth. Chronic diseases can result in a loss of self-esteem, as individuals may feel as though they can no longer participate in activities that once brought them joy and fulfillment.

Additionally, chronic diseases can result in a loss of purpose and meaning, as individuals may feel as though they can no longer contribute to society in meaningful ways.

The relationship between chronic disease and depression is complex and multi-factorial. It is influenced by a range of physical, psychological, and social factors.

Addressing these factors and providing support and resources for individuals with chronic disease is essential in reducing the risk of depression and improving mental health.

This may include access to mental health services, emotional support, financial assistance, and rehabilitation services. By addressing the relationship between chronic disease and depression, we can help individuals to live healthier, happier, and more fulfilling lives.

***

There is a significant gender difference in the rates of depression in the United States, with women being diagnosed with depression at much higher rates than men.

This disparity in depression rates between women and men is a complex and multi-factorial issue that has been the subject of much research and debate. Understanding the reasons for this gender difference is vital in addressing and reducing the burden of depression in the United States.

One of the primary reasons for the gender difference in depression rates is the impact of hormonal changes on mental health. Women experience a range of hormonal changes throughout their lifetime, including puberty, menstrual cycles, pregnancy, and menopause, which can impact their mental health and contribute to feelings of sadness, anxiety, and irritability.

Another factor contributing to the gender difference in depression rates is the impact of stress and life events. Women are more likely to experience stressful life events, such as relationship problems, financial difficulties, and the care of children and elderly relatives, which can contribute to feelings of sadness and hopelessness.

Additionally, women are more likely to experience gender-specific forms of stress, such as sexual harassment, domestic violence, and discrimination, which can contribute to feelings of anxiety and depression.

A third factor that contributes to the gender difference in depression rates is the impact of social and cultural norms. Women are often expected to be caretakers and nurturers and may feel overwhelmed and stressed by the responsibilities of caring for others.

Finally, the gender difference in depression rates may also be influenced by differences in help-seeking behaviors and access to mental health services.

Women are more likely to seek help for mental health problems and are more likely to access mental health services. In contrast, men are more likely to ignore or deny their symptoms and may be less likely to seek help.

Gender differences in depression rates are a complex and multi-factorial issue influenced by various physical, psychological, and social factors. Addressing these factors and providing support and resources for women are essential in reducing the burden of depression in the United States.

This may include access to mental health services, emotional support, financial assistance, and resources to address gender-specific forms of stress and trauma. By addressing the gender difference in depression rates, we can help women to live healthier, happier, and more fulfilling lives.

CHAPTER 7
Covid, homelessness, and burnout

Special considerations are warranted concerning the increased rates of depression associated with the unprecedented global pandemic, rising rates of homelessness, and burnout.

The coronavirus (COVID-19) pandemic has significantly impacted the mental health of people in the United States and worldwide. The pandemic has brought about widespread stress and uncertainty, creating new challenges and hardships for many individuals.

Studies have shown that the pandemic has led to increased rates of depression and anxiety, as well as increased symptoms of post-traumatic stress disorder (PTSD) and other mental health conditions. The pandemic has also disproportionately impacted specific populations, such as essential workers, people of color, and individuals with pre-existing mental health conditions.

Further, there is data to support the increase in rates of depression due to the coronavirus (COVID-19) pandemic in the United States. The pandemic has significantly impacted mental health, with many individuals experiencing increased levels of stress, anxiety, and depression.

According to a recent study by the Centers for Disease Control and Prevention (CDC), approximately 41%

of adults in the United States reported struggling with mental health or substance abuse during the pandemic.

This incidence is a significant increase in mental health problems compared to pre-pandemic levels, with nearly 1 in 4 individuals reporting symptoms of depression and anxiety.

Additionally, the pandemic has resulted in various stressors, including financial insecurity, job loss, and social isolation, which can contribute to depression and other mental health concerns.

The impact of the pandemic has also been particularly pronounced among certain populations, including essential workers, individuals with pre-existing mental health conditions, and communities of color.

The COVID-19 pandemic has profoundly impacted mental health in the United States, with many individuals experiencing increased levels of stress, anxiety, and depression.

The pandemic has resulted in a range of stressors, including financial insecurity, job loss, and social isolation, which can contribute to depression and other mental health concerns.

Isolation and uncertainty that have characterized the pandemic have been particularly challenging for many individuals. They have contributed to increased rates of depression.

Regarding the relationship between a COVID-19 infection and depression, evidence suggests that individuals who have contracted the virus may be at an increased risk of depression. The physical and emotional toll of a severe illness can be substantial.

Individuals who have recovered from COVID-19 may continue to experience symptoms such as fatigue and difficulty concentrating, which can further contribute to depression.

The relationship between COVID-19 and depression is complex and multifactorial. The stress and uncertainty of the pandemic, as well as the impact of the pandemic on physical health, social support, and economic stability, all contribute to increased rates of depression.

In terms of suicide, it is still too early to determine the full extent of the pandemic's impact on suicide rates.

However, initial data suggests that there may have been a rise in suicidal thoughts and behaviors among some individuals during the pandemic.

Factors such as job loss, financial stress, social isolation, and increased substance use have increased suicide risk.

It is important to note that the effects of the pandemic on mental health and suicide are complex and multi-faceted and that further research is needed to understand the impact of the pandemic on these issues entirely.

The pandemic has also created new challenges and hardships for many individuals and may have contributed to increased suicide risk.

It is important to continue to invest in mental health and suicide prevention efforts and to provide support and resources for individuals who are struggling with mental health challenges during these difficult times.

***

There is a strong link between homelessness and

depression. Homelessness is a complex and multi-faceted issue that can significantly impact a person's mental health.

The stressful and uncertain living conditions associated with homelessness, the loss of social support networks, and increased exposure to trauma and violence can contribute to depression and other mental health problems.

Studies have shown that homeless individuals have a higher risk of developing depression compared to the general population. This is likely due to the accumulation of stress and trauma associated with homelessness and the lack of access to adequate mental health services and support.

Homeless individuals may also experience various physical health problems, including malnutrition, exposure to harsh weather conditions, and infectious diseases, which can further contribute to feelings of hopelessness and helplessness.

The stigma and discrimination associated with homelessness can further contribute to feelings of shame, guilt, and worthlessness, which can contribute to the development of depression. Homeless individuals may also experience a sense of hopelessness and helplessness due to the difficulties of finding stable housing and employment, which can further contribute to feelings of sadness and despair.

There is a strong link between homelessness and depression; addressing this issue is essential in improving mental health outcomes for homeless individuals. This may involve providing access to mental health services and support, improving access to affordable housing and employment opportunities, and addressing the root causes of homelessness, such as poverty and economic inequality.

By addressing the link between homelessness and depression, we can help to reduce the burden of depression and improve mental health outcomes for this vulnerable population.

***

There is a relationship between burnout and depression. Burnout is a state of emotional, physical, and mental exhaustion that results from prolonged and chronic stress. It is characterized by cynicism, detachment, and a reduced sense of personal accomplishment.

Depression, on the other hand, is a mental illness characterized by persistent sadness, hopelessness, and a loss of interest in activities that were once enjoyable. It can also be accompanied by physical symptoms such as fatigue, sleep disturbances, and changes in appetite.

Understanding these differences can help to improve the prevention, early detection, and treatment of burnout and depression.

The risk of burnout and depression can vary by age. Young adults, particularly those in their twenties and thirties, may be at a higher risk of burnout due to the demands and stressors of entering the workforce and establishing their careers.

Older adults, particularly those in their fifties and sixties, may also be at risk of burnout and depression due to the demands of caring for aging parents, financial stressors, and the upcoming retirement years.

Gender also plays a role in the risk of burnout and

depression. Studies have shown that women are at a higher risk of burnout and depression than men. This may be due to women's additional demands and stressors, such as balancing work and family responsibilities and dealing with gender-based discrimination and bias.

Women are also more likely to seek help for mental health concerns, which may contribute to the higher rates of depression in women.

Occupation can also play a role in the risk of burnout and depression. Individuals who work in high-stress, high-demand occupations, such as healthcare, finance, and law enforcement, may be at a higher risk of burnout and depression due to the demands and stressors of their work.

Additionally, individuals who work in low-paying, low-status occupations may also be at a higher risk of burnout and depression due to a lack of control, autonomy, and social support.

The current rates of burnout in the United States vary by age and gender. However, burnout has become increasingly prevalent in recent years due to the demands and stressors of modern life.

According to recent studies, burnout is most common among young adults, particularly those in their twenties and thirties. This is likely due to the demands and stressors of entering the workforce and establishing their careers.

Young adults may be at a higher risk of burnout due to the increasing use of technology and social media, which can contribute to feelings of overwhelm and stressed.

Women are also more likely to experience burnout compared to men. This may be due to women's additional demands and stressors, such as balancing work and family responsibilities and dealing with gender-based discrimination and bias. Women are also more likely to seek help for mental health concerns, which may contribute to the higher rates of burnout in women.

Studies have shown that individuals who experience burnout are at a higher risk of developing depression. This may be due to the fact that burnout and depression share similar symptoms and underlying causes, such as chronic stress, a lack of control, and a lack of social support.

Burnout can lead to a sense of hopelessness and helplessness, which can further contribute to the development of depression.

Furthermore, burnout can also have a negative impact on physical health, which can further exacerbate feelings of sadness and despair. For example, individuals who experience burnout may experience fatigue, sleep disturbances, and changes in appetite, which can further contribute to feelings of hopelessness and helplessness.

There is a relationship between burnout and depression, and addressing burnout is essential in reducing the risk of depression. This may involve improving work-life balance, reducing stress, and providing support and resources to individuals at risk of burnout.

By addressing burnout, we can help to reduce the burden of depression and improve mental health outcomes for individuals in the United States.

CHAPTER 8

Suicide – a tragic consequence of depression

Suicide rates have increased over the past several decades in the United States. In 2020, the suicide rate was 14.9 per 100,000 individuals, a 15% increase from 2000.

Suicide rates tend to be highest among older adults, particularly those over the age of 65. In 2020, the highest suicide rate was among individuals aged 45-54 years (20.9 per 100,000 individuals).

Concerning gender, suicide rates tend to be higher among men than women. In 2020, the male suicide rate was 26.9 per 100,000 individuals, while the female suicide rate was 6.2 per 100,000 individuals.

With regard to race, suicide rates tend to be highest among non-Hispanic white individuals. In 2020, the suicide rate among non-Hispanic white individuals was 17.8 per 100,000 individuals, while the suicide rate among non-Hispanic Black individuals was 7.1 per 100,000 individuals.

While trends and patterns in suicide rates can provide some insight into the issue, it is important to consider the available data's limitations and challenges and continue to invest in research and prevention efforts to address this serious public health issue.

***

What is the most common reason for suicide in America? How can this be addressed in both a proactive manner and treatment of mental disorders?

Suicide is a serious public health issue in the United States and a leading cause of death among Americans. The most common reason for suicide is mental illness, particularly depression and other mood disorders. Other factors contributing to suicide risk include substance abuse, trauma and abuse, relationship problems, and financial stress.

To address the issue of suicide proactively, awareness and understanding of mental health issues are essential. Also, providing resources and support for individuals struggling with mental health challenges is crucial. This support can include community-based programs and initiatives and public education campaigns to raise awareness about mental health and the warning signs of suicide.

In terms of treatment for potential mental disorders, individuals need to seek help if they are experiencing symptoms of depression or other mental health issues. Treatment options for depression and other mental health conditions include therapy, medication, and support groups. Therapy can help individuals understand and manage their emotions. It can provide them with coping skills and strategies for managing their symptoms. Medication can help alleviate symptoms of depression and other mental health conditions, and support groups can provide individuals with a sense of connection and support.

It is also important for individuals to be aware of the warning signs of suicide and to seek help if they or someone they know is experiencing suicidal thoughts or behaviors.

Warning signs of suicide can include changes in mood or behavior, increased alcohol or drug use, withdrawal from friends and family, and feelings of hopelessness or helplessness.

***

Depression is a major risk factor for suicide. It is estimated that up to 90% of individuals who die by suicide have a diagnosable mental health condition, including depression.

Depression is a complex and debilitating illness that can affect a person's thoughts, feelings, and behaviors. When left untreated, depression can lead to feelings of hopelessness and helplessness and increase the risk of suicide.

Suicide is most likely to occur when individuals are experiencing the most intense symptoms of depression, such as hopelessness, worthlessness, and a loss of interest in life. Other factors that can increase the risk of suicide include a history of previous suicide attempts, a family history of suicide, access to firearms, and a recent life stressor, such as a relationship breakup or job loss.

The best way to prevent suicide is to address the underlying causes of depression and other mental health conditions and to provide individuals with the support and resources they need to manage their symptoms.

Prevention strategies can include therapy, medication, support groups, community-based initiatives, and public education campaigns to raise awareness about depression and suicide prevention.

It is also important for individuals to be aware of the warning signs of suicide and to seek help if they or someone they know is experiencing suicidal thoughts or behaviors. Warning signs of suicide can include changes in mood or behavior, increased alcohol or drug use, withdrawal from friends and family, and feelings of hopelessness or helplessness.

No one is immune to depression or the tragic consequence of this disease, suicide. Regardless of wealth or economic status, suicide is a dreaded consequence of having a turbulent emotional state and depression.

No evidence suggests that wealthy people commit suicide more frequently than poor people. Suicide is a complex and multi-faceted issue influenced by many factors, including mental health, life stressors, and access to resources.

While some research has suggested that individuals with higher education and income levels may be at lower risk for suicide, other studies have found no relationship between socioeconomic status and suicide. Additionally, some research has suggested that individuals with higher education and income levels may be more likely to attempt suicide but less likely to die by suicide.

It is important to note that suicide is a complex issue influenced by many factors and that socioeconomic status is just one of many variables that can contribute to suicide risk. Other factors, such as mental health, life stressors, and access to resources, can play a much more significant role in determining suicide risk.

Suicide is a complex issue influenced by many factors, including mental health, life stressors, and access to resources. By addressing these underlying factors and providing support and resources for individuals struggling with mental health challenges, we can work to prevent suicide and promote emotional well-being for all individuals, regardless of socioeconomic status.

While it is true that women are diagnosed with depression more frequently than men, the suicide rate is indeed higher for men than for women. There are several reasons why this disparity exists:

1. Different methods of suicide: Men are more likely to use violent methods of suicide, such as firearms, which are more lethal than the methods typically used by women, such as overdoses.

2. Undiagnosed depression: Men may be less likely to seek help for depression and may be less likely to receive a diagnosis of depression compared to women. This can lead to a lack of treatment and support for depression, increasing the risk of suicide.

3. Stigma and cultural norms: Cultural norms and stereotypes may discourage men from seeking help for mental health problems and view depression and other mental health conditions as a sign of weakness. This can lead to a reluctance to seek help and a lack of recognition of depression and other mental health conditions in men.

4. Life stressors: Men may be more likely to experience specific life stressors, such as job loss, financial stress, and relationship problems, which can increase the risk of depression and suicide.

In summary, while women are diagnosed with depression more frequently than men, the suicide rate is higher for men due to a combination of factors, including different methods of suicide, undiagnosed depression, cultural norms, and life stressors.

By addressing these disparities and increasing access to mental health resources, we can work to improve the emotional well-being of all individuals and prevent suicide.

PART III
**Dealing with Sadness
and
Treating Depression**

CHAPTER 9

*Tips and suggestions for combating
social and life issues that can make
you cry, sad, or depressed.*

Dealing with sadness, crying, or depression can be a complex and challenging experience. Still, several strategies can help you manage these emotions and promote emotional well-being.

Whether you are dealing with life stressors, social issues, or persistent sadness, the following tips and suggestions can help you find hope and happiness and overcome challenges.

1. Connect with others: Building and maintaining strong social connections are integral to emotional well-being. Spending time with friends and family, participating in community activities, or joining a support group can help you feel less isolated and provide a sense of connection and support.

2. Practice self-care: Self-care is essential to managing your emotions and promoting overall well-being. Self-care can include engaging in physical activity, eating a healthy diet, getting enough sleep, and doing things you enjoy.

3. Challenge negative thoughts: Negative thoughts and beliefs can contribute to feelings of sadness and depression. Challenge these thoughts by questioning the

evidence for them and looking for evidence that supports a more positive perspective.

4. Seek professional help: If you are experiencing persistent sadness or depression or your emotions affect your daily life, it is vital to seek professional help. A mental health professional can help you develop coping strategies, provide support and guidance, and offer treatment options.

5. Practice mindfulness: Mindfulness is a technique that can help you focus on the present moment and reduce feelings of stress and anxiety. Mindfulness can include meditation, deep breathing, and mindful movement.

6. Focus on the present: It can be easy to get caught up in worries about the future or regrets about the past, but focusing on the present can help you manage your emotions and promote a sense of peace and well-being.

7. Find meaning and purpose: Having a sense of purpose and meaning in your life can help you manage your emotions and promote emotional well-being. Discovering your life's purpose can include pursuing a passion, volunteering, or setting and working towards meaningful goals.

8. Build resilience: Resilience is the ability to bounce back from adversity and is an integral part of emotional well-being. Building resilience can involve developing coping skills, seeking support, and focusing on positive experiences.

9. Get active: Physical activity is vital to emotional well-being. It can help you manage your emotions and promote peace and well-being. Becoming more active can include engaging in physical activity, such as exercise or yoga, or simply spending time in nature.

10. Practice gratitude: Gratitude focuses on what you

are thankful for. It can help you manage your emotions and promote emotional well-being. This can include keeping a gratitude journal, expressing gratitude to others, or focusing on positive experiences.

Dealing with sadness, crying, or depression can be a complex and challenging experience. Still, several strategies can help you manage these emotions and promote emotional well-being.

The tips and suggestions outlined above can help find hope and happiness and overcome challenges, whether dealing with life stressors, social issues, or persistent sadness.

By focusing on self-care, connecting with others, and practicing mindfulness, you can build resilience, find meaning and purpose, and promote emotional well-being.

***

What is the role of resilience in combating sadness or depression?

Resilience is the ability to bounce back from adversity and is integral to managing sadness and depression. Resilience is like a superhero power, providing individuals with the strength and courage to face difficult emotions and experiences and to emerge from them stronger and more resilient.

Imagine a world where sadness and depression are as common as the rain. These emotions come and go, sometimes in gentle showers, other times in torrential downpours. But amid this emotional storm, there is a superhero, a beacon of hope, a force to be reckoned with. This superhero is called resilience.

Resilience is the ability to weather the storm, rise above the darkness, and find the light. It is the power to face and overcome adversity, to find hope and happiness in the face of difficulty. Resilience is not just a skill. It is a mindset, a way of looking at the world and seeing the possibilities, even during the storm.

Resilience is like a shield, protecting individuals from the harmful effects of stress and adversity. It helps individuals to manage their emotions and to find meaning and purpose in the face of challenging experiences. With resilience, individuals can face their feelings head-on and find the courage and strength to overcome them.

Resilience is also like a compass, guiding individuals toward their goals and dreams and helping them to navigate their emotions and experiences. With resilience, individuals can find their way through the storm and emerge stronger and more resilient.

Resilience is not just a superhero power but a way of life. It is the ability to find hope and happiness, even in the face of adversity. It is the power to overcome sadness and depression and to find joy and fulfillment in life. Individuals can find meaning and purpose and build a rich and fulfilling life with resilience.

*****

What is the difference between faith, religion, and spirituality? How does each play a role in promoting mental health?

Faith, religion, and spirituality are related but distinct concepts that can promote emotional well-being and mental health.

Faith refers to a person's beliefs and values and can be a source of comfort, support, and hope. Faith can give individuals a sense of meaning and purpose and offer a framework for understanding the world and their place in it. Faith can also help individuals manage their emotions and experiences and provide them with a sense of peace and comfort.

Conversely, religion refers to a specific set of organized beliefs and practices associated with a particular faith or spirituality. Religion can give individuals a sense of community and belonging and offer opportunities for spiritual growth and personal development.

Religion can also provide individuals with guidance and support in managing their emotions and experiences and offer a framework for understanding the world and their place in it.

Spirituality refers to a person's sense of connection to a higher power or the world around them. Spirituality can provide individuals with a sense of meaning and purpose and offer a framework for understanding their emotions and experiences.

Spirituality can also offer a sense of peace and comfort and provide individuals with a sense of connection to something greater than themselves.

Faith, religion, and spirituality can provide a sense of meaning and purpose by offering a framework for understanding their emotions and experiences. They can also give individuals a sense of community and belonging and provide opportunities for spiritual growth and personal development.

***

How can we decrease the rates of depression in America?

While there is no single solution to decreasing the rates of depression in America, several strategies can help reduce the burden of depression, including increasing access to mental health resources, reducing stigma, and improving the quality of care.

One of the key strategies for decreasing the rates of depression in America is increasing access to mental health resources. This includes making mental health services more affordable and accessible, particularly for uninsured or underinsured individuals.

Expanding public health insurance programs, such as Medicaid, and implementing policies that increase access to mental health services, such as telehealth and mental health integration into primary care.

In addition to increasing access to mental health resources, reducing the stigma associated with depression is critical to decreasing the rates of depression in America. Stigma can prevent individuals from seeking help for depression and can make it more challenging to diagnose and treat depression.

Strategies for reducing stigma include educating the public about depression and its impact on mental health, promoting positive media portrayals of mental health conditions, and engaging in public speaking and media campaigns.

Improving the quality of care for individuals with depression is another important strategy for decreasing the rates of depression in America. This includes training healthcare providers to be culturally competent and to understand the unique experiences and challenges faced by different populations, such as African Americans and older adults.

It also includes integrating mental health services into primary care, such as through co-located clinics or integrated care teams, and using evidence-based treatments, such as cognitive-behavioral therapy and medication management, to treat depression effectively.

Another important strategy for decreasing the rates of depression in America is investing in research to understand the causes of depression better and to develop new and more effective treatments. This includes funding research into the biological, psychological, and social factors that contribute to depression and into the development of new and innovative treatments, such as transcranial magnetic stimulation and teletherapy.

Finally, addressing the social determinants of depression, such as poverty, stress, and lack of access to resources, is critical to decreasing the rates of depression in America. This includes implementing policies and programs that address poverty and inequality, promoting healthy behaviors and lifestyles, and providing access to supportive services, such as housing, food, and transportation.

***

What's the future of mental health prevention,
early detection, and treatment in America?

The future of mental health prevention, early detection, and treatment in America is rapidly evolving. New technologies, innovations, and best practices are emerging to improve the lives of individuals with mental health conditions.

One of the most significant trends in the future of mental health is the integration of mental health into primary care. This involves integrating mental health services into general medical care, such as through co-located clinics or integrated care teams, to improve access to mental health resources and improve the quality of care for individuals with mental health conditions.

This trend is driven by the recognition that mental health is an integral part of overall health and that early detection and treatment of mental health conditions can prevent more severe and debilitating conditions from developing.

Another key trend in the future of mental health is the use of technology to improve access to mental health resources and the quality of care.

Delivering mental health services remotely through video conferencing and other technology can improve services. Wearable devices, such as smartwatches and fitness trackers, to monitor mental health and well-being can also help keep the patient connected to needed care.

Technology can make mental health resources more accessible and convenient. It can help to reduce barriers to care, such as stigma, lack of access, and cost.

Evidence-based treatments, such as cognitive-behavioral therapy and medication management, are also a key trend in the future of mental health in America.

Evidence-based treatments are the most effective and efficient way to treat mental health conditions. These treatments can be customized to meet each patient's individual needs.

The future of mental health in America will likely involve continued investment in research to develop new and innovative treatments and to improve the delivery of existing treatments.

Another important trend in the future of mental health is recognizing the importance of addressing the social determinants of mental health, such as poverty, stress, and lack of access to resources. This includes implementing policies and programs that address poverty and inequality, promoting healthy behaviors and lifestyles, and providing access to supportive services, such as housing, food, and transportation.

By addressing these underlying social factors, we can help to prevent the development of mental health conditions and improve the overall health and well-being of individuals with mental health conditions.

Finally, reducing the stigma associated with mental health conditions is critical to the future of mental health in America.

This includes educating the public about mental health and its impact on overall health, promoting positive media portrayals of mental health conditions, and engaging in public speaking engagements and media campaigns to reduce stigma and increase awareness.

CHAPTER 10

Do current medications for depression work?

The effectiveness of medications for the treatment of depression is a complex and highly debated issue in the field of mental health.

While some medications effectively treat depression, others have been highlighted for their lack of efficacy and potential side effects.

Antidepressant medications, such as selective serotonin reuptake inhibitors (SSRIs) and tricyclic antidepressants (TCAs), have been widely used to treat depression for several decades.

These medications work by altering the levels of neurotransmitters, such as serotonin, in the brain, which are thought to be involved in regulating mood and emotions.

Studies have shown that these medications can effectively treat depression, particularly in individuals with moderate to severe depression. They are often prescribed in combination with psychotherapy.

However, despite their widespread use, there is an ongoing debate about the efficacy of these medications for the treatment of depression. Some studies have found that these medications are no more effective than a placebo, and their benefits are primarily due to the placebo effect.

Additionally, these medications can have serious

side effects, including weight gain, sexual dysfunction, and increased risk of suicide, which can limit their use and effectiveness in treating depression.

In recent years, there has been growing interest in alternative treatments for depression, such as ketamine-based treatments and psychedelic-assisted therapies.

These treatments have shown promise in early studies, particularly for individuals with treatment-resistant depression. They are thought to work by changing the neurochemical and neurobiological processes contributing to depression.

However, more research is needed to fully understand these treatments' efficacy and determine their long-term safety and effectiveness.

The current state of medications for depression is complex, and there is an ongoing debate about their efficacy and safety.

While some medications, such as SSRIs and TCAs, are effective in treating depression, others have been criticized for their lack of efficacy and potential side effects.

Alternative treatments, such as ketamine-based and psychedelic-assisted therapies, show promise. Still, more research is needed to understand their efficacy and safety fully.

Ultimately, the decision to use medications for depression should be based on carefully considering the individual's specific needs and symptoms and in consultation with a mental health professional.

CHAPTER 11

Are there alternative medical or herbal therapies for depression?

While traditional antidepressant medications are widely used to treat depression, they may not be adequate or suitable for everyone. As a result, there has been increasing interest in alternative medical and herbal therapy treatments for depression.

One of the most promising alternative treatments for depression is acupuncture. This traditional Chinese medical practice involves the insertion of thin needles into specific points on the body to stimulate the flow of energy or Qi.

While the exact mechanism by which acupuncture works is not yet fully understood, it is thought to directly impact the central nervous system and affect the release of neurotransmitters, such as serotonin and norepinephrine, which are involved in regulating mood and emotions.

Several studies have shown that acupuncture can effectively treat depression, particularly in combination with other treatments, such as psychotherapy and medications.

Another treatment for depression is omega-3 fatty acids, essential fatty acids found in high concentrations in fish oils and other fatty fish.

Omega-3 fatty acids are thought to affect the release

of neurotransmitters. They have anti-inflammatory effects, and several studies have shown that omega-3 supplements can be effective in reducing symptoms of depression.

However, more research is needed to fully understand the efficacy of omega-3 fatty acids as a treatment for depression and to determine the optimal dose and duration of treatment.

Herbal therapy is another alternative treatment for depression. Several herbs, including St. John's Wort, ashwagandha, and saffron, have been studied for their effects on depression. St. John's Wort, in particular, has been widely used as a natural remedy for depression and is as effective as some antidepressant medications in treating mild to moderate depression.

One of the most promising alternative medical treatments for depression is transcranial magnetic stimulation (TMS).

This non-invasive procedure involves using magnetic fields to stimulate nerve cells in the brain. TMS is effective in treating depression, particularly in individuals with treatment-resistant depression.

It is thought to work by altering the release of neurotransmitters, such as serotonin and norepinephrine, in the brain.

Finally, exercise and physical activity have also been effective in treating depression. They are often recommended as an adjunctive treatment for depression. Exercise is thought to work by increasing the release of endorphins, which are natural mood-enhancing chemicals, and by improving the overall functioning of the brain and central nervous system.

In addition, physical activity can help to reduce

stress, improve sleep, and increase overall well-being, all of which can help to reduce symptoms of depression.

Alternative medical and herbal therapy for depression offer promising alternatives to traditional antidepressant medications. They can effectively treat depression, particularly in individuals with mild to moderate depression.

These alternative treatments may not be suitable for everyone and should be used in consultation with a healthcare professional.

By exploring the available alternative medical and herbal therapy treatments for depression, individuals can find the right treatment for them and improve their emotional well-being.

CHAPTER 12

A final plea to America and the world:
How can we, as a society, decrease
the rate of suicide?

To decrease suicide rates, we must take a comprehensive approach that addresses the multiple factors contributing to suicide, including access to mental health resources, reducing stigma, improving the quality of care, and addressing the social determinants of suicide.

One of the most critical strategies for decreasing suicide rates is increasing access to mental health resources, including affordable and accessible mental health services.

Reduced rates of suicide can be achieved by expanding public health insurance programs, such as Medicaid, and implementing policies that increase access to mental health services, such as telehealth and mental health integration into primary care.

Improved mental health support services will help to ensure that individuals with mental health conditions receive the care they need to prevent suicide and manage their symptoms effectively.

There are several strategies for reducing the stigma associated with having a mental health diagnosis. Educating the public regarding mental health's impact on overall health is essential.

Further, promoting positive media portrayals of mental health conditions and the importance of taking the appropriate steps to maintain or treat mental health illnesses will reduce the stigma associated with behavioral health diseases.

Improving the quality of care for individuals with mental health conditions is another important strategy for decreasing suicide rates. This includes training healthcare providers to be culturally competent and to understand the unique experiences and challenges faced by different populations, such as African Americans and older adults.

Integrating mental health services into primary care, such as through co-located clinics or integrated care teams, and using evidence-based treatments, such as cognitive-behavioral therapy and medication management, to treat mental health conditions effectively will promote wellness, identify disease, and enhance treatment.

An essential strategy for decreasing suicide rates is investing in research to understand the causes of suicide better and to develop new and more effective treatments. This includes funding research into the biological, psychological, and social factors that contribute to suicide and into the development of new and innovative treatments, such as transcranial magnetic stimulation and teletherapy.

Finally, addressing the social determinants of suicide, such as poverty, stress, and lack of access to resources, is critical to decreasing suicide rates. This includes implementing policies and programs that address poverty and inequality, promoting healthy behaviors and lifestyles, and providing access to supportive services, such as housing, food, and transportation.

By addressing these underlying social factors, we can help prevent the development of mental health conditions and improve the overall health and well-being of individuals at risk for suicide.

Decreasing suicide rates requires a comprehensive approach that addresses the multiple factors that contribute to suicide, including access to mental health resources, reducing stigma, improving the quality of care, investing in research, and addressing the social determinants of suicide.

Working together to address these challenges and increase access to mental health resources, we can improve the emotional well-being of all individuals and prevent suicide.

Suicide Prevention Resources

"988" is the three-digit, nationwide phone number to connect directly to the 988 Suicide and Crisis Lifeline.

By calling or texting 988, you'll connect with mental health professionals with the 988 Suicide and Crisis Lifeline, formerly the National Suicide Prevention Lifeline.

Veterans can press "1" after dialing 988 to connect directly to the Veterans Crisis Lifeline, which serves our nation's Veterans, service members, National Guard and Reserve members, and those who support them. For texts, Veterans should continue to text the Veterans Crisis Lifeline short code: 838255.